Book!

You Know What You Ought to Do Is Read This Book!

The Life and Times of a Modern Day American Gypsy

By A.P. Eman

The contents of this work, including, but not limited to, the accuracy of events, people, and places depicted; opinions expressed; permission to use previously published materials included; and any advice given or actions advocated are solely the responsibility of the author, who assumes all liability for said work and indemnifies the publisher against any claims stemming from publication of the work.

Dorrance Publishing Co
585 Alpha Drive
Suite 103
Pittsburgh, PA 15238
Visit our website at *www.dorrancebookstore.com*

ISBN: 979-8-88604-674-8
eISBN: 979-8-88604-758-5

It was it was the middle of the 20th century on an early fall morning when God said let there be light. OK so it wasn't the beginning of time, but it was for me. It was the late 50s when I was born on a military base in Florida, a spot made popular by the TV show, "I Dream of Jeannie." Born to a young officer and his younger wife I already had an older brother who was born two years earlier.

Six weeks later my dad gets transferred to another base in Florida, in five more moves from Florida all the way out west to California, and back east to North Carolina in four years I get another brother. During my younger years that I don't remember we had a German shepherd that ended up dying at an early age from rat poisoning. My mother has told me a story of when I would play in the gravel behind the house, the dog Andy would sit next to me and nudge me to come in when my mother would call, and that I would grab Andy by the tail to make him sit back down, but he eventually made me go in.

I have also seen pictures of myself in Disneyland, the Grand Canyon, and in Mexico during this period of my life, but I was too young to remember. Now in North Carolina, and the middle child my parents started me in kindergarten a year early so my mom could concentrate on the baby. This stop is where I develop my first real memories, one of which is how many times I had to have stitches. The first time I had stitches was in my hand, and after the Novocain wore off my hand just throbbed with pain.

Every time I cut myself after that I had the core men at the base hospital stitch me up without Novocain, I became known in that hospital as the kid that doesn't take Novocain. Now I'm only four or five years old, which is a little young for sexual experiences, but I and the little girl next door were caught with our pants down in her carport when her mother got home. The girl's mother swore to my mother that I was out to get her daughter. My older brother and myself were caught jumping out of a tree with our pants down in front of some girls from the neighborhood, we would jump out of the tree into a roll of wire fencing that had leaves in it so the girls couldn't see us on the ground.

Our mother knew of it when we got home, and we got punished. This stop is also where I remember sliding under a fence behind our house and walking to the general store with my brother and friends where we would buy sodas. I was the only one in the group who liked Mountain Dew, it's when they're ads depicted a hillbilly saying, "Yahoo Mountain De it'll tickle your innards, I drink diet Dew now. My older brother and I got along great having survived a gas leak in base housing on a prior base. That base happened to be in Roswell NM, so that gas leak was probably some type of alien experimentation on us military lab rats.

Well, that's my excuse, and I'm sticking with it. My older brother once fell out of a tree from about 20 feet up, I was standing on the ground when he landed after hitting his chin on a branch. He was knocked unconscious, his chin badly cut with pine needles sticking in the cut. I ran through the forest, and up to the house yelling," mommy, mommy Jimmy's dead," that's the fastest I've ever seen my mother move. Although she once chased me down before I made it under the fence when the doctor made a house call, and I knew I was going to get a shot. Several years after my younger brother was born, we were on the move again.

In two more moves, and before my dad spends a year in Vietnam, I find myself in Texas again when I am about 10 years of age. This time I'm old enough to remember visiting Monterrey Mexico, the first time I remember seeing the startling difference in the way the third world lived. While my dad was in Vietnam, we lived in Louisville Ky so my mom could be near her family, when we lived right down the street from my cousins.

We were only there for a year, so I went to the second half of 5th grade and the first half of 6th grade there. This is where I first remember smoking cigarettes, my mom would send us to the store for cigarettes with a note that we would change from one to two packs, they were only $0.26 a pack so it was easy to scrape up the extra money. We would then take our pack to the creek where we would smoke them, and then get sick, my older brother would end up getting caught smoking while we were camping out in the backyard.

While we were in Louisville I played baseball on the same fields, and in the same Babe Ruth organization that my son would play in 20 plus years later. This is also where I remember stopping at McDonald's while walking home from school and buying a chocolate milkshake for $0.25. When my dad gets home from Vietnam we go back to Ohio, where after finishing up 6th grade I found myself starting junior high school. In the next three years I will experience my first real sexual encounters and smoke my first marijuana when I am 13 or 14.

In Ohio junior high school was 7th, 8th, and 9th grade, and I still had not reached 5 feet in height, so I had little self-confidence, especially when it came to girls. I remember my math teacher in one of my classes asking this beautiful blonde who was about five feet seven if she would consider going out with someone of my stature. Of course, she said no, she looked at me and said nothing personal. Yeah, nothing personal! I was a popular guy, a wrestler because I was small, and the wrestling coach asked me to join the team. I was also the class clown, so I did not let it show how much it hurt, but it didn't help my confidence heading into high school.

The traveling when we were on the move between bases was not the only time we spent on the road during these years. We did a lot of traveling by car between our homes and my grandparents in Louisville Ky, a lot of our vacations were spent with my grandparents. In the back of the station wagon, yelling "are we there yet," on small highways most of the time because there were very few freeways at the time. Small mountain roads through tunnels, across dams and bridges across gorges, traveling back then was much more adventurous than it is these days on freeways.

When we weren't traveling by car, we'd be in a small airplane because my dad was a pilot, and he could rent a plane from the base. A couple of our Christmas vacations that I remember were spent with my grandparents in Miami Beach FL. My uncle who was head of marketing for the Florida Citrus Commission would get us tickets to the Orange Bowl football game and get us into shows at Disney World without having to wait in line. It was our Christmas vacation in 1972 in Miami when we were having lunch at a restaurant, I finished early and went out to the car to listen to the radio when I found out that baseball great Roberto Clemente had died in an airplane crash.

I had been a baseball fan almost all my life and baseball would play a big part later in my life. From listening to the Cincinnati Reds on the radio, and getting a scorecard signed by Pete Rose with some other old time Reds in 1968, to coaching my son for several years later in life. I have digressed enough, high school is about to start, and 10th grade started with a bang, and the beginning of a lifelong inability to make a good decision.

Before the first high school football game a couple of friends and me drank a gallon of homemade grape wine. The alcohol did not hit me until I was in the football game. All I could remember was sitting in the bottom row of the end zone seats puking my guts out. A youth minister from a local church was helping me when the police stepped in and took me out to their car. They laid me on the hood of the police cruiser where I continued to throw up on the car before the cops pulled me off and dropped me on the parking lot.

While the police called my parents, I tried to escape by crawling under the police car before my dad arrived. I didn't get punished too badly; the hangover was bad enough. The high school allowed me to wrestle if I stayed out of trouble. While that was my first foray into to drinking, I had already smoked pot several times with the first being when I was 13 or 14. The first time I can remember being really stoned was with my best friend in the 10th grade. We went with a mutual friend to his dealer's house where we smoked in a pilot's oxygen mask, we were so stoned that we could not quit laughing and the guy asked us to leave.

Now as a 15-year-old sophomore who is barely 5 feet tall, I had no clue when it came to girls. I was popular with the cheerleaders though, one who was my height liked me, but she was two years older than me, so I thought she was just teasing me. Early in the morning of a big tournament the cheerleaders would get our parents to let them in the house before we got up and decorate our bathrooms. The cheerleaders also used to give me rides home after school or after wrestling practice, and when they dropped me off, they would dare me to moon them, and I would not disappoint them. It wasn't until I told her I was moving to Florida because my dad was retiring that I realized the short cheerleader really did like me.

I hadn't had much experience with women. I had once met a girl I liked at a party when I was in the 9th grade, we spent the entire party making out in the dark. When I saw her at school, she told me she was forbidden to see me because her mom saw the hickeys I put on her breasts when she came out of the shower. I also spent a couple of hours in an old spring cellar with an older more experienced girl, and I got my hand in her pants, and a hand job from her.

My only other sexual experiences were getting my finger stinky underneath a blanket on the bus going to church camp, and while at camp. Also getting busy with the girls in the basement of the church, (Baptist girls are wild), pretty much sums up my entire education of the opposite sex. This church is also where I met one of my best friends, we would hang out after church until choir practice and yes, I used to try to sing but I was never really very good at. We would get something to eat, and usually go to a movie or just hang out until later.

One rainy Sunday after church we sat through three showings of The Outlaw Josey Wales. He was one of the first people I smoked pot with. Moving to Florida is going to give me a clean slate, I would overcome my insecurities, and thrive. My life was just beginning, my aunt cut my hair as it had become wavy, and hard to manage so she gave me an afro style. So, it was off to a sleepy little beach town in Florida, making my 13th move, and sixth school system in 15 years, but this was the first school system I will have been in that had black students, because Florida had been busing for a few years already.

At first, I was the only white student with an afro so, I got along with most of the black students as they referred to me as curly. On the morning of my junior year photos, I woke up late with my long curly hair a mess, I threw on a ratty T shirt and got stoned on my way to school. My mother really hated that picture, she wanted me to get it retaken but I never did. There was an incident during black history week of my junior year when some of the black students started a riot by beating up two white girls, one of which was a foreign exchange student.

The police arrived before a crowd of white students could confront the black students. The students that beat the two girls got arrested, but the rest of the black students were loaded on school buses and taken home. That only happened in my junior year, but something of a more personal nature happens in my senior year. Now that I've gotten ahead of myself, I'll start with my first day in Florida. While I was sitting at a desk in our front yard, in the middle of summer taking inventory of furniture, and boxes coming off the moving van, the girl next door stopped by to say hello.

She was a dirty blonde beauty with big tits, and her T shirt had the picture of a guy with his face melting, and the caption said, "stoned again." She asked me if I wanted to get high when I was done. There was a large tree between our houses where we met and got high for the first time, and many times thereafter. Although nothing ever happened between us, I used to watch her sunbathe in the nude on top of their motorhome from this tree.

We would get high at the bus stop before school, then we would go to the traffic island in front of the school after arriving on the bus and get high again. I remember once walking into homeroom late as the teacher was closing the door, and as I was squeezing through the door, I was saying good morning when I burped in his face, and a puff of smoke came out right in his face. The teacher said to me "I thought you were a wrestler," I am I said.

He asked me why I smoked cigarettes if I'm a wrestler, and I said I don't smoke cigarettes. A friend of mine who was in my homeroom just started laughing, and the teacher asked him what was so funny, but he just said nothing. I bought a motorcycle from a guy down the street from us for $100, it was an older Honda CL 175 that I rode to school with my best friend riding bitch, he was a freshman who was in my science class and on the wrestling team.

It was his house where I met my first Florida girl. I was 16 with a motorcycle, and a Volkswagen bug, and this girl lived across the street from my best friend, and she was a 19-year-old woman with a child, but she liked me. We would have sex on her bed with her one-year-old daughter asleep in the bed right next to us, we also managed to have sex in the back of my Volkswagen bug. A few months with an older more experienced woman taught me a lot for when I got my first real girlfriend, whom I met when a friend and I skipped school and went to the beach instead.

She was a beautiful blonde a little taller than me with a nice figure, and big boobs who really loved sex. I remember once lying on top of her naked, still inside of her, and a friend of hers knocks on the bedroom door, and just walks in on us. Of course, both girls screamed as if embarrassed to death. We also once had sex in our swimming pool while my mother was in the kitchen making dinner. It was the 70s, and it seemed like everyone was having sex.

A friend on the wrestling team who had a good job and made good money would pay when we would go out to the red-light district. I think he paid because he didn't want to go alone, my high school best friend went with us once, and chickened out not wanting to lose his virginity to a prostitute. Well, my junior year was getting close to ending, so I signed up for Babe Ruth baseball, little did I know it would be my last year playing baseball.

It was cool playing on the same field pros played on during spring training. I was still barely over 5 feet tall, so I didn't play much, but when I did, I impressed most everybody, I was small but extremely athletic. I once flied out to the warning track and went first to third on a single in my sparse appearances. My best friend, who rode bitch on my motorcycle went back north to live with his dad after school let out, so that summer was mostly spent with my girlfriend when I wasn't working. I was a busboy/dishwasher at a local steakhouse, and even though I had a girlfriend, I had a major crush on one of the waitresses, she was shorter than me, and gorgeous. She was older than me and married though, but I tried, the most I got was some kissing.

Now I've been in Florida a little more than a year when my senior year begins. One day at school, this guy I knew who, "was the guy" to buy weed from asked me if I knew where to get some weed, I thought that I had arrived. I have a nice car, a girlfriend, a job, and a reputation. My life could not be any better. School was a breeze compared to the high school in Ohio. When not at work or school we were on the beach throwing the frisbee for hours on end.

Back in the 70s there were no sun blocks, so the girls on the beach were glistening brown beauties covered in baby oil. I remember one girl in particular; she had a beautiful dark brown tan and wore either a brown or yellow bikini. Whenever she would walk by, I would say hello and walk with her for a while if she was alone but, as much as I tried, she always shut me down. Then came Hawaiian Tropic, and Panama Jack, SPF 1, and SPF 2, and so on as they discovered how harmful too much sun can be.

People who grew up here from a very young age before sun blocks are more likely to develop skin cancer, or just happen to look older than their years, especially if they didn't take care of their skin. From the tiny bikinis at the beach, to the Daisy Dukes, and halter tops the seventies were dripping with sex. Before he went to live with his dad, or maybe it was after he came back, my best friend and I were in my car near the red-light district.

While stopped at a traffic light a beautiful young black woman with small tits approached my window braless in a white tank top with big hard pokies. She asked me for three dollars, I offered her $5 to pull up her shirt and wiggle her beautiful tits in my face. She accepted, and my buddy went wild laughing while calling me a crazy little son of a bitch. On the weekends if we weren't at the beach, we'd be out on my dad's boat which was an 18-foot runabout with an 85 horsepower Evinrude motor water skiing. We also tried it naked, and we called it skeaking.

We would take the boat upriver where the water was smooth and fresher, but there were alligators laying on the banks so if you fell you had to be quick to get back in the boat. The boat had two six gallon gas tanks, and we could run all day on those. If we did need to get gas it was only $0.50 a gallon at the marinas. At night we would go to the rock pits, which was an old rock quarry right behind the Southside drive in theater. We could watch and listen to the movies from the rock pits for free, while drinking beer and skinny dipping in the freshwater lakes, and it's amazing there were never any alligator attacks.

With my high school best friend living up north with his dad, my life got a little boring as my girlfriend kept me out of trouble that summer. Although there was one night in the skating rink parking lot where we guys waited for the girls to finish skating. We had had a little bit of beer to drink that night, so when the police showed up, they determined that I sounded too tipsy to drive, so they called my parents. This is the same parking lot where my high school best friend and myself got three rednecks to back down after they would confront us a couple of years later.

That was it for suspense in my life, my senior year is just breezing along. Wrestling season is going well, and at weigh ins for a match, the guy from one of the neighboring schools who I pinned in 28 seconds a year earlier, offered to split a half pound of weed with me if I didn't pin him, I pinned him anyways. I started my senior wrestling season at 119-pound weight class, and during the season when I would get to school in the morning, I would go to the student union building to get a Mountain Dew and M&M's from the vending machines. That would be it for the day except for some Gatorade at practice until I got home and would have a cube steak and a salad for dinner.

Over the Christmas break all the weight classes go up two pounds, so I went down to 114-pound class, and two other wrestlers on the team also dropped a weight class. The next match we really surprised their wrestlers with who they were facing. My season went well, made it all the way to the regional semifinals, and I had a partial scholarship offer to wrestle in college, but in two weeks things change dramatically.

I was out with friends one night, drinking beer which I didn't like so I only had about a beer or two all night. We were just out driving around all-night siphoning gas so we could stay out longer, and I had told my parents I was sleeping at a friend's house. At 3:00 AM I decided to drive home, but I never made it! My parents got a phone call from someone who said I'd been in an accident behind their house.

The fact is I had fallen asleep at the wheel and sped into a palm tree at 70 mph, and I was not wearing my seat belt causing me to be thrown into the back seat breaking my neck. Palm trees are very hard, the royal palms have been described as concrete poles with little green trees on top of them. The palm tree I hit is still here, but so am I. The steering wheel hit me in the face and broke my jaw in two places, with the bone protruding through the inside of my mouth, badly cutting my tongue to where the doctor was not sure he could save it.

The front left tire came through the floorboard and broke my left ankle, I also had a double concussion, and a hernia which the doctor said would heal naturally, but it didn't. After the doctor sewed up my tongue it swelled up to block my breathing, so the doctor performed a tracheotomy so I could breathe. After my parents received the first phone call, they got a call from the police confirming their fears. The police had still not gotten me out of the car when my parents drove by the accident. By the time the doctors got to look at me, and my X rays they saw the break was so high up on the spine they told my parents that I would be dead by morning.

I was in ICU for eight days with my neck in traction with just a 10% chance of survival because the break was so high. The neck keeps swelling for 8-10 days after a break, and they were worried the swelling would push the bone into the spinal cord and cut it. The break was so high that if it did cut the spinal cord, it would have killed me, so while in traction they had me tied down with restraints to keep me from moving around and trying to get out of bed. I don't remember the first eight to 10 days I was in the hospital, so I don't remember any of this happening, but my mother told me that I broke several sets of restraints, so they put two restraints on each arm and each leg, and I broke one of the rails off the bed.

Like I said, I don't remember any of this happening, but my mother told me that she asked me why I was being obstinate, and I told her that if they would untie me, I would settle down, and I did. My being in excellent condition and having a strong neck from wrestling is what saved my life. I was in the hospital for a total of eight weeks, and with 7 weeks in traction. My jaws were wired together for six weeks, and the hospital puree diet was nasty, so I lived on tomato soup and chocolate malts while in the hospital, and my weight went from 130 pounds to 103 pounds.

Whenever my parents, girlfriend, or friends would come over they would bring me a chocolate malt from Dairy Queen. My girlfriend put some Chef Boyardee ravioli in a blender, and I tried to drink that through a straw, but it didn't work very well. I'm not sure if it was the drugs I was on, but I kept the room very cold, and would lie in bed shirtless with the sheet down around my waist. Whenever my girlfriend, or my mom and other women visited they wore sweaters.

One time when the doctor was visiting, he saw a nurse slap my foot and tell me to uncross my feet. The doctor said to let him cross his legs, that I was a 17-year-old boy who was injured not sick, and not an old person with poor circulation. After six weeks they unwired my jaws by pulling the wires out of my gums between each tooth, and without Novocain it was the most painful experience of my life. Two weeks later I am released from the hospital wearing a neck brace that the doctor said I would have to wear for six months.

In just six weeks the doctor let me take the brace off, and he was really surprised that it healed so quickly. Out of the hospital, and back in school with my neck brace on. I had missed a lot of school, and my art teacher was going to flunk me, so my guidance counselor talked to the teacher for me, and the teacher said," oh I thought you were just a sophomore, don't worry about it." I passed art with a B and went to the prom with my neck brace on. Graduation comes, and the long, strange trip continues.

While I was still in the hospital my best friend who moved away had come back. He and I were partners in crime, not real bad crime, just fun loving, mischievous young men. Like going into a cow pasture early in the morning after a heavy rain, looking for "MAGIC" mushrooms that grew up right out of the cow shit. These are called Psilocybin Mushrooms and have a gold circle on top, and a purple ring around their stems, and that's why they're called Gold Tops or Purple Ringers. You must get mushrooms before the sun comes up because they are mostly water, and the sun will burn them up.

My best friend and some of the other guys I'd go with would pull a mushroom out of a pile of shit, brush the shit off and eat it right there in the field, that would make me puke. I would wait till we got home and make tea out of it. From all the drugs, the drinking, and all the casual sex, this is the continuation of my lifelong inability to make a good decision. From my two DWI's, and a very short stay in the Air Force I was struggling with the fact that my life was never going to be easy.

I was way too immature to have joined the Air Force, and my girlfriend who had broken up with me said she wanted to get back together before I left for basic training. I was too insecure, and jealous to handle my emotions, and was not liking the military life. The hernia I had from the accident never healed, and it strangulated one night causing me to go to the hospital. I received an honorable discharge under medical conditions. The month or so that I was in basic training I ran into two people from earlier in my life, one was a guy I had been roommates with one summer at wrestling camp and got kicked out of camp with me for getting caught sneaking out of the dorm one night.

I had gone to that same wrestling camp the summer before and snuck out of the dorm the last two nights to spend with a girl I had met in town. The other was a girl I knew in junior high and high school in Ohio, talk about a small world. After my discharge I went home to my girlfriend, and she proceeded to break up with me. No Air Force, and no girlfriend I had surgery to repair the hernia, and I got a job at a store in the mall.

When I wasn't working, I'd either be at the beach or a bar looking for women. Every week there would be a keg party somewhere, we'd have big keg parties out behind the airport, and sometimes hundreds of people would show up. At a party at a friend's house one night, I was sitting in a chair, and this beautiful blonde who was my high school best friend's ex-girlfriend came over and sat on my lap and said let's get out of here and have a party of our own. We got in my car and took a drive out behind the airport, and we were laying on a blanket under the stars with her shirt open, with her beautiful braless breasts glistening in the moonlight when I hear this voice in my head telling me she's still his girl.

I apologized to her and told her I couldn't do it because my best friend still liked her. She really was one of the most beautiful girls I've ever known, but I was loyal to my friend. He and I had once bought a gram of crystal tea and sold enough to go to the Foghat concert in Miami. It was Rick Derringer, and Johnny Winter who opened for Foghat, and we were so fucked up I had to break the rear window of my car after the concert because I had locked my keys in it.

I then find out that he had already slept with my ex, so I lied to my best friend about having sex with this girl he liked. He will save my ass once later though when I "borrow" a car from my ex-employer, a car rental company that I had worked for. I wore my company jacket to the car dealership that serviced the rental company's vehicles and I got in one and drove off. That night my best friend and myself were driving around when he decides he wants to drive the car, and while he is driving, he makes a U turn in the middle of the road and a cop pulls us. I had an Ohio driver's license, so I told the officer that my parents had rented the car for me while I was down visiting and that I left the contract on the dining room table.

Because I didn't have the contract with me, they towed the car. The next day I went to the car rental place that I had worked at to pick up some personal items I had left there and stole a no-show contract that I used to get the car out of impound and return it to the rental company. Because my friend could not prove he had insurance on the car at the time he had to pay for extra insurance for a year or so. But that was better than getting busted for a stolen car. Well, high school has been over for a while, I'm not in the Air Force, and the next six or seven years are quite the strange trip indeed.

A couple of DWIs Wrapped around chasing after an old girlfriend in Ohio. A DWI is, "driving while intoxicated." My first DWI was while driving my 65 GTO I had bought for $500 from the mechanic at the Exxon station I worked for on Sanibel Island, and the police also found a bag of marijuana in my car, so I was arrested and taken to jail until my dad arrived to get me out. My GTO was a beautiful red car with black vinyl interior, but it burned oil very badly. After taking the GTO to a concert in Tampa the car started making a loud tapping sound coming from underneath the hood.

I was working at a different gas station at this time, so I decided to drive the car right to the station, and into the service bay to begin tearing the engine down. So, after I finished rebuilding the engine, I decided to sell the car, and buy a newer car to go after the old girlfriend in Ohio. While in Ohio I lived with my brother and his wife, and the girl I was chasing had no interest in me, couldn't blame her though, I was an immature kid with little self-confidence working at a gas station.

While living in Ohio, I went to the band "Yes in the Round" concert, I ate two hits of blotter acid, and snorted 1/3 of a gram of cocaine before the concert and was smoking pot inside the concert because pot had been decriminalized in Ohio back in the 70s. The wildest concert I ever saw, and I'm not sure anybody else saw the same concert I saw. But I would go on to see the band Yes in the next two decades also. My very first concert was when I was a kid, my parents took us to see the original Jesus Christ Superstar rock concert, but I digress.

It's no wonder why the girl, or any girl wasn't interested in me, I had no clue of how to treat women, and I'm still not very good at it today. Back then girls were for dating and fun not much else. Once I was in the mall when I was around 17 or 18 to do some shopping, and everywhere I went this same cute girl would always be there. I approached her and asked if she was following me. She said she was following me, so we went back to my place to have sex. My younger brother was at home, so I told him to let me know if mom or dad came home.

One time I had decided to hitchhike to the beach when this old station wagon pulled over to pick me up. There was a guy driving and two girls in the front seat when I got in the back, one of the girls jumped into the back seat, put her arm around me and asked me what my name was, before I could answer the driver says you're supposed to ask him how old he is first, so she asked me how old I was, and I told her I was 19. She said good you're not jailbait and put her hand on my crotch. We went to the beach and smoked their pot, and they bought all the beer that day. I had sex in the back of the station wagon with one of the girls on our way to her boyfriend's house so she can make him lunch.

I had to walk home because the driver of the car caught me with his girlfriend in the other bedroom, but that was okay because it was a good day. Cute girls were everywhere, and eager to please. So why I ever went after her in Ohio is a mystery, I had no plan, little education, and a total lack of understanding life or women. After figuring out she was not interested in me I continued working at the gas station, this was the late 70s when gasoline went from $0.35 a gallon to $0.70 a gallon.

There were gas wars and rationing going on, but our station had the lowest prices in town. We sold gas, oil by the quart, cigarettes, milk, and 16-ounce glass bottles of soda, all at the lowest prices in town. We were always busy, so I wore a changer on my belt, and I became good with numbers in my head. We had an African foreign exchange student working for us, and as smart as he was, he had no common sense. Someone would give him a dollar for a 52-cent pack of cigarettes, and he would go use the adding machine.

A short time later another customer gives him a dollar for a pack of cigarettes, and he goes to the adding machine again. Another guy I worked with at the gas station showed me how to have surf and turf at McDonald's. You would take a cheeseburger patty and put it on your fish sandwich to make surf and turf, it's really pretty good. But, working at a gas station was not going to get me the girl, or any girl for that matter. There were a couple of young women who would hang out around the gas station that I dated, but no relationship lasted because of my immaturity and insecurities.

With my life starting to spiral out of control my brother did not want me around anymore. He got my parents to get me to move to my aunts in Kentucky, and work for my uncle. My uncle was a concrete contractor, the hardest job I have ever had, digging up rock and clay, and having to push a wheelbarrow when short in height is difficult because you must bend your arms.

This situation only lasted a couple of months being that I used and abused any, and all who offered to help. So, after burning bridges in Ohio and Kentucky my parents get me home, and I hook up with an ex-wrestler friend who was a couple years older than me. His dad's house had a swimming pool that nobody cleaned, and the water was dark green, we would swim in it anyways, and play tag naked with girls we would pick up.

One night I was having sex with a girl on the dining room floor when his father came out of the bedroom and walked right past us into the kitchen and got in the refrigerator, and then he just walked back into his room and shut the door. The next morning, he made a comment about coming out of his room and seeing all these moons laying around on the floor. The friend and I decided to get an apartment together, the apartment we got had a loft with windows that overlooked the roof.

This is when I found out that he liked to run drugs with a needle, I myself never used a needle, I would snort whatever he would shoot up. One night tripping we got on the roof and walked across the complex to this window of a woman's apartment, and we were talking to her through her window. She didn't have a problem with us doing that, but her boyfriend who was the director of a local gymnasium, and an ex-boxer called the police on us and got in a fight with my friend in the hallway to the apartments.

We were arrested and spent the night in a holding cell where we could reach through a hole in the wall, and into a storeroom where we pulled out pieces of a fake Christmas tree that we put up in the holding cell. After this episode is when my parents decided to send me to "Outward Bound" to build my self-confidence. Little did they know how their decision to send me would affect my life. Two weeks in the mountains rock-climbing, white-water canoeing on the river the movie "Deliverance" was made on and spending three days and nights in the mountains by myself gave me some insight, but what happens after is the real life changer.

Two or three weeks in the mountains together with a small group of people you build bonds with some more than others. One young woman and I built a friendship, and when it came time to leave, we only had $13 between us, so we decided to hitchhike to the airport, and we got into an older 2 door Bronco with me getting in the front with the driver. After the driver started drinking vodka, he drove us up onto the Blue Ridge Parkway despite us repeatedly telling him to stop and let us out with him saying if he lets us out, he won't get what he wants.

The Blue Ridge Parkway is a federal road that is patrolled by federal officers called Parkway police. It runs through the Appalachian Mountains, built so that they could move military equipment through the mountains. When we turned on to the Blue Ridge Parkway I told the guy, "If you're not going to take us to the airport just let us out now," and he said that he would let us off in three miles, and I told him to stop the truck right there and let us out.

That's when he came across with a backhand and hit me in the face, and when he tried to hit me again, I caught his right arm and was struggling with him in the front seat when the woman I was with reached from the backseat and was able to turn the key off. When the truck came to a stop close to a rock wall, I got out with my walking stick and backpack while trying to pull the woman out at the same time, but the driver had hold of the woman's jacket sleeve trying to keep her in the truck.

I beat his windshield out with my walking stick while he was getting his truck restarted. The woman's foot got stuck in the doorway of his truck, causing me to get knocked down and her to be dragged 75 feet. When I ran over to her, she was lying on her back on the side of the road with her eyes rolled back in her head, blood and pus coming out of her ears which are both signs of a concussion. When I got to her, she was talking, but it was gibberish, so I stood up and watched him speed down the road past a Parkway Police car, and when he drove past them their lights were on, so I just waved my arms at them to go after him.

They turned their car around and went after him, when they caught up to him, he had pulled off to the side of the road and jumped down a 15-foot embankment through trees and bushes trying to escape into the woods, but one of the officers, an older white-haired gentleman got out and pumped his shotgun once, and the guy wouldn't move, but he wouldn't come out of the woods either. He stayed in the woods screaming, "they kidnapped me, they tried to rape me." Five police officers had to go down into the woods and tie a rope around him to drag him up out of the woods, one of the officers said they couldn't fit both of his hands around the guy's bicep.

The police also found a knife and a handgun in his car along with the half empty bottle of vodka. It turns out the Parkway police saw everything that happened from the time I jumped out of the car, and they were wondering what was going on. He was a short stocky farmer who we put away for 15 years on two counts of kidnapping, and a count of assault resulting in serious bodily injury. The woman I was with recovered from her injuries, and when we went back for the trial the officers told us of a double murder from a year earlier this guy had been tied in with.

Even with the drama, the time I spent on Outward Bound caused me to fall in love with the Appalachian Mountains so much that is where I decided to go to college. Before I went to college though, I would spend a couple of years working at a local department store with the guy that will become my all-time best friend. We'd always be partying all night and go straight to work without sleep.

We would go to work at six or seven in the morning, and one of these mornings after partying all night we took our morning break and went out to the car to snort some cocaine we had saved to keep us going through the rest of the day. I cut the coke up on an 8-track tape and set the tape on the center console, and my buddy had just emptied his ashtray and put the ashtray back when he blew the ashes away, but he also blew the cocaine into the carpet. Needless to say, we were bummed out and tired.

One night when I was out alone at a local Disco bar on ladies' night when I saw this good-looking brunette sitting alone so I asked her to dance. While dancing I told her that if she was interested, I had some cocaine we could do, and she said we could go to her office. She was a dental hygienist and we had sex in the dental chair. It was the first time that I cleaned the hygienist's teeth. This is about the time I got my second DWI, and I was also ticketed for driving on a suspended license.

I had been out partying all night when the bars closed at 2:00 A.M., and I went to a bottle club where I ran into my friend's ex who had sat on my lap at a party and continued to drink with her. Around 5:00 A.M. I took her home, but all I remember is dropping her off, I don't remember driving the 8 or 10 miles home across the river, past my road, and into somebody's backyard with my front tires hanging off the seawall. The next thing I remember is standing in the yard looking at my car wondering how it got there, I got back in the car and tried to back it off the seawall, but it wouldn't move, so I went around to the front of the house to see if I could use their phone.

Still drunk, instead of ringing the doorbell, I just opened the door and walked in, when realizing that I shouldn't have walked in I went back out and rang the doorbell. When the homeowner came to the door I asked if I could use his phone, and he said I could after he called the police. I called my dad, and he got there about the same time as the police. I go to jail again; my dad comes and gets me out. My first morning at work after being in jail, a coworker had a copy of the local newspaper that had a picture of my car hanging off the seawall with the caption saying that I picked a peculiar place to park.

At my court appearance, because I had also been ticketed for driving on a suspended license the judge suspended my license for six years saying I was a habitual offender, and I was also sentenced to 10 days in the county stockade. I told the judge that I had a good job with vacation time coming up, and he told me I could report for jail on a certain date at 5:00 P.M. It was a Wednesday after work my buddy was going to take me to jail, and we stopped by a friend's apartment where I drank a Dixie cup of mushroom juice before going to jail.

After I was booked in I had quite a night tripping in jail, the stockade is several fenced in dormitories that had about 16 prisoners each locked in. I sat in the corner of the dorm pretending to read a book while trying not to freak out, because everybody's faces looked cartoonish. The next morning a couple of the guys in jail with me asked me what was wrong with me the night before, so I told them that I had been tripping on mushrooms, and they thought I was crazy. After 10 days in jail, and even though my license was suspended for six years I continued to drive, and I went back to work at the department store working on the loading dock, and with housekeeping.

One morning I was vacuuming women's fine clothing when I went into the changing room, I see the buyer from Miami standing there in her bra and underwear. Not startled at all, she asked me how she looked as she took off the bra to put her blouse and skirt on. She then came over to me give me a kiss on the cheek and gave my aroused crotch a pat before making me promise not to tell anybody about that morning. There were a couple of other women that worked there that

I had relations with, and some others who I just flirted with hoping to get further. One night a couple of coworkers from the loading dock had a party with a keg of Heineken, I got so drunk the last thing I remembered was passing out on the couch.

I woke up in bed underneath a woman I knew from work with me still inside of her, with her smiling face just inches from mine. This woman had a fine body, but she was not someone that I was interested in, so I just pushed her off rolled over and went to sleep. It was a Sunday morning and Father's Day when I woke up, while getting dressed she asked me where I was going, and I told her I had to get my father something for Father's Day.

She then asked me if I'd be going to the beach later and I told her that yes, I probably would be going to the beach. She then asked me to take her to the beach with me, but I made up an excuse to why I couldn't do that. Two things I remember most about working at the department store, other than the women, was how heavy the first Amana Radaranges were, and how dirty the women left the women's bathroom. I mostly worked, partied, and chased women for two years before I decided to attend the highest major university in elevation on the East Coast. Boy was that a blast, and I am not talking about school. Grandfather mountain acid trips were the best, camping under the stars in the mountains is so incredible, high or not.

Watching the sun come up over the clouds is awe inspiring. I really love those mountains, and the times I had in them. A rope swing into a frigid mountain stream where the most fun was watching the pokies as the girls got out of the frigid water. One night at a party at a cabin on the side of a mountain we ran out of beer, so tripping our lights out we decided to go on a beer run. While driving down a small winding mountain road listening to Rick Wakeman's "Journey to the Center of the Earth," we encountered some pea soup fog. I was looking down out of my driver's window at the stripes in the road because I could not even see the front of my car, and we were on a very narrow winding mountain road.

Needless to say, we took the main roads back to the party. After the party ended, at around 7:00 in the morning, still spacing out I drove to said rope swing, not to swim but to collect my thoughts. As I sat on a rock by the mountain stream, a butterfly landed on the rock about two feet away from me with a little puddle of water between us, but he was looking right at me. As the butterfly was looking at me, and I was looking at him, I was saying and thinking to myself, come here little butterfly, come here.

As I sat there with my arms around my knees, that butterfly walked across that rock with the wind blowing it's wings sideways, and through the puddle, onto my shoe, up my pant leg, and onto my arm where he sat and stared at me until the wind blew him away. I know y'all probably think I was just hallucinating, but I swear it really happened. At another party that we all went to out of town at a friend's parents' house Is where I lost it.

While tripping on acid and drinking beer I blacked out after getting in the hot tub naked with some other people, and I got out of the hot tub to get a beer without putting any clothes on. I then got back into the hot tub alone and I would go underwater and stay underwater for as long as I could, and when I would come up out of the water, I would run my hands through my wet hair as I would gaze up at the stars and gasp, "WOW!" One friend, who was an anarchist had gone to the party with us claimed that I was regressing like William Hurt in the movie "Altered States," and he came over to the hot tub to get me out when he realized I had already gotten out of the hot tub and was running around the woods naked howling at the moon.

When he found me, I was leaning against a streetlight naked waving at the cars as they passed by, he then tried to get me to put my pants on when I hit him. One of the girls who went to the party with us came out and got me to put my pants on and took me back to the party. I don't remember any of that episode, after climbing into the hot tub I just blacked out. Then there was being in the right place at the right time.

Like once when we all went on a hike through the woods, and we stopped at a bench along the trail to take a picture. So, while most of the group were sitting on the bench looking at the camera, I was standing on the far end of the bench mooning the girl with the camera. Nobody knew of me mooning her until her slideshow a week or so later. You all do remember slides, don't you? I once took a picture of a dead rabbit on the side of the road, and at my slideshow I told the girl I had mooned that I had a picture of a bunny rabbit sitting on the side of the road.

She was not happy when she saw the dead rabbit. She was the same girl that got me to put my pants on at that party. We were probably the two leaders of our little group even though we were two very different people, I was classic, and she was punk rock. I remember her and I once went on a hike by ourselves with our cameras and stopped to take a rest. She was lying on her back in long green grass as I laid next to her on my side up on my elbow, I almost leaned over to kiss her, but I didn't, and it was just a short time later that she would meet the founder of an underground newspaper.

With all the fun there wasn't much time for classes, but I learned a lot from the couple of the guys in the group who started the underground newspaper, they opened my eyes to politics, one guy in the group was the aforementioned anarchist, and he could not believe that I wrote a poem when I read it to the group, because I came from a conservative military family. Years later one of my poems would be published in a poetry contest. One day I was at the anarchist's apartment when his girlfriend got there. He and his girlfriend excused themselves and went into the bedroom and closed the door, before I left, I went to his stereo and put the Rolling Stones song, "She Comes in Colors" on, and turned it up loud so they could hear it in his room. The apartment I lived in with two friends was," The Twilight Zone apt U2." The apartment was above a beauty shop, so we figured that we lived above beauty.

This was after my first year of college when at the age of 22 I had lived in a freshman dorm partying and playing backgammon instead of going to classes. One day while sitting in my dorm is when I found out John Lennon had been shot. Because I was of legal age, I would buy beer and liquor for the others, and in exchange they would pay for mine. I should have gone to summer school after my first and only year, but instead, I went out to Spokane WA with the Southwestern Book company to sell books door to door.

We had a caravan of 5 or 6 cars going to Spokane, but my car kept breaking down. I had gotten some bad gas and my fuel filter kept getting clogged. Cars were easy to work on back then, so at one stop I was able to buy some extra fuel filters to use as needed. One time when it broke down and I was installing a new filter this long-haired bearded guy walked up and asked me for a ride to a seminary in Colorado. He then asked me if I mind that he prayed for my car, and I said it couldn't hurt. So, he put his hands on the hood of my car and he prayed for it, but it did break down again with him in the car, and he got a ride with somebody else while I was working on my car.

While hauling ass through Montana trying to catch up with the rest of the group, I got pulled over for speeding twice within 5 minutes, but each time I just had to pay the officer $5 because Montana was fighting the 55 mile an hour speed limits imposed by Jimmy Carter. When I finally get to Spokane selling books did not go well, so in two weeks I'm working for a guy who had bought a rundown ranch. He hired me to help get his house ready to sell, and the ranch ready to move on to. While I was working for him, I met his granddaughter who lived in Seattle, so I spent a week with her, and we went up to Vancouver for a weekend. I also traded my Camaro type Lt for a Mazda RX2, it was a very fast little 4 speed with a Rotary motor.

All in all, it was a pretty good trip out west, but because I didn't go to summer school I couldn't get back into school, and when I checked my campus mailbox there was a letter from one of the girls in our group. She was the youngest in our group, an 18-year-old platinum blonde with smokey eyes, nice perky tits, and just a tiny overbite. She was so hot; I would flirt with her as I would sit behind her in my roommates Volkswagen van I would kiss and nibble on her neck when her boyfriend wasn't around. By the time I got back from Spokane, she and her boyfriend had gotten back together, once again I missed out on my chance to get the girl.

At first, I stayed with three girls rent free while keeping their apartment clean for them. I slept on their hide a bed, and it saw quite a bit of action because I had relations with two of the girls I was living with. I'm sure they knew about each other, but the best looking one who was a beautiful blonde would let me climb into bed with her, but just for some cuddling and some kissing because she had a boyfriend. One of the girls took me to her home for Christmas, and her hot little sister would not leave me alone. Other than these two girls I lived with there were a few other girls in the mountains that I had relations with.

One in particular would call me whenever she needed something like a ride home, or if she just wanted a good fuck. She was as horny as she was beautiful, and we actually had sex one night in a cemetery. One night after she and I had sex she asked me if she could borrow my car because she wanted to go home to see her boyfriend, I told her

I would drive her if she would pay for the gas. I spent the weekend with her and her boyfriend, and she introduced me to a girlfriend of hers, a beautiful little redhead.

There were four or five of us there and we were all doing blotter acid, the redhead and I had been making out in a beanbag so everybody else left the room, and as we continued and I pulled her pants down I saw her bush and commented on it being red, she said, "what did you expect," when we finished having sex and walked outside the group of friends were waiting and applauded us as we exited. As good as things seemed I was not doing very well in night school, and I never got back into college.

The one good thing to come out of night school was a girl I met, it didn't last long because she was serious about school, and I wasn't. I was at a party one night when I saw one of the most beautiful women I've ever known, sitting on the couch talking to some guy when I went over, stood next to the couch, and started talking to her. She stopped talking to the other guy, and when he got up to go get her a beer, she asked me to sit down in his place to talk. She didn't go to school there as she was in town to visit a friend of hers, so we went to her friend's apartment.

Her friend was someone I had slept with, and I had told her that I felt like I did her a favor when I slept with her, she then kicked me out of her apartment undressed. This girl I was with asked me if I had told her friend that I thought I had done her a favor, and I told her yes, I did, and that I regretted doing so. Her friend returned to the apartment while we were getting undressed and kicked us both out of the apartment, we ended up going back to my place and spending the night together.

I also went to see her in her hometown on my way back to Florida before going to Europe for a few months with a couple friends to do some snow skiing in the Austrian Alps along with partying and sightseeing with the locals. We flew from Miami to London England, and to Brussels Belgium where we got on a train that went along the beautiful Rhine River with castles on the hilltops, to Ulm West Germany. I was awake for the train ride as I slept on the airplane, whereas the other two partied on the airplane and slept on the train.

One of the guys I went with was, and still is my best friend, he was born in Zurich Switzerland. His mother was born in a small farming town in West Germany near the Black Forest, and where we stayed with his uncle was only an hour and a half from the Austrian Alps. We went skiing almost every weekend we were there. The resort we stayed at was mainly for the local people, it wasn't a big tourist trap. We could ski down the mountain all the way to where we were staying, and the place we stayed in only cost us $8 a night each. There were about five people staying in the room we were in, and we had to go to the end of the hallway to use the bathroom, but it was great.

Other than skiing we did some sightseeing, we went to Zurich, and Munich while we were there. There were a couple of girls while I was in Europe, and one was a local girl who had a boyfriend who was hoping I would go home soon. The other girl was a young woman I met in a bar while out partying with the locals, and she came home and spent the night with me before she got up the next morning and left hitchhiking her way across Europe. In the spring when ski season was winding down, all the little farming communities had their spring dances for the young people, and as soon as we showed up at the dances everybody knew there were Americans there, or as they called us Ammies.

We got in a fight with jealous boyfriends at almost every dance we went to. We were in our early 20s, and the German girls our age all spoke English because they continued their schooling. The boys in these farm communities usually quit school after the 6th grade and went to work on the farm, went to a trade school, or into the military. So, the girls at the dances all wanted to dance with us and talk to us about America, and that got the guys jealous. I've got a scar on my chin where a guy hit me with a big square ring, but I got the better of him by bleeding all over him.

At the last dance in the town we were staying in, I was sitting on a table talking to the local girl who liked me while her boyfriend sat on the other side of her, and he had no clue to what we were talking about. We were making plans for later that night after she took her boyfriend home we would meet up and go parking near the Black Forest. After three months in Germany, I learned enough German to get by, and the girls would translate for us if necessary. The locals would say my German got better the more I drank.

As good as the beer was, and as fun as the girls were, skiing through waist deep Austrian powder was even better. Up in the Alps the snow would fall so heavily that if you were in a bar for four hours there could be up to a foot of snow on the roof of your car, snowflakes big enough to knock you down. Before ski season was over one Saturday morning I had a real bad sore throat, but one of the locals stopped by and asked if anyone wanted to go skiing, and in my scratchy voice I said hell yes.

It ended up being a really warm day on the slopes, so girls were wearing just their ski bibs with nothing underneath, talk about side boob. Women were lying in lawn chairs at the top of the mountain soaking up sun, and it was such a nice day that I just wore a sweater with my ski bibs with a scarf around my neck. I also drank four or five Jager teas which are like a Long Island iced tea served hot with a slice of orange, and the fumes made my eyes water.

But my sore throat went away, and when they closed the slopes at 5:00 P.M. we stayed on top of the mountain partying with the workers at the ski resort who we had come to know through the ski season. Then just before dark we had to ski down the mountain, or more to the point fall down the mountain. About a month before we were planning to leave, I was almost out of money, and so was my best friend.

One of the local women got us jobs at a local landscaping company, and we would get up in the morning have a cup of instant coffee and catch a bus to the next town where the company was. On our first day of work, we got in the company truck with the crew, and drove for a while before stopping, and being told to stay in the truck. The foreman and one other guy went in the store and came out with five or six cases of beer to take to the job site, and one guy had a beer open as soon as they got in the truck.

The crew got a kick out of us because we were either drinking water or coke instead of beer. The first job we were on was building some cement stairs on a college campus. Stairs in German is treppe, being on a college campus we decided to call the stairs "preppy treppe." The second job we were on was building a winding sidewalk out of interlocking bricks about 200 yards long up a slight hill.

On this job, for lunch we sat at on a hillside overlooking a beautiful valley with this small German town. We worked for three weeks making pretty good money. It was 1982 and they were paying us $360 a week. Our foreman wished we weren't leaving because we were his best workers, of course we were the only ones not drinking beer. As beautiful as it was, there was no more skiing, and I was ready to go home.

So, my best friend's cousin took us to Ulm West Germany to catch the train to Brussels Belgium and fly home. It was funny when we ordered a Budweiser on the plane, and they came in 12-ounce cans. The cans seemed so small because all the beer in Germany came in half liter bottles, and the Budweiser tasted like water after all the German beer, and that's why the Germans call it," Budwasser." Now before we get home to Florida, we have a 6-hour layover in London. So, we get to bum around London for a few hours, and had some fish and chips while looking for Abbey Road. While we never found Abbey Road there were penny slot machines all over London, and my best friend won almost every time he played a slot, I never won. After a 6-hour layover we are almost to the end of our most awesome trip.

When we get to the airport in Miami, and we get a rental car, when we first get in the car my friends noticed a smell coming from the back seat, which is where I'm sitting. The smell happens to be the Puma running shoes I've been wearing the entire three months, with the same socks on this entire trip home. I take off my shoes and socks and tie them to the rack on top of the car while washing my feet off in a puddle and keeping my feet out the window until they dry. They smelled so bad the guys were making jokes that the cars behind us were swerving out of the way from the smell.

Three hours later and the trip is over. I go back to North Carolina to try to start my college life again, but it never happened. I was working at a restaurant during that summer while using a friend's car, after that car broke down, I quit my job, and decided to hitchhike to Jekyll Island GA chasing after the girl I had met at the party. But she had a boyfriend, and I did not figure into her future, so not getting the girl again I hitchhiked back.

As I was hitchhiking on the highway a pickup truck pulled over to pick me up, and as I was walking up to the truck It looked like the driver was alone when somebody else sat up in the truck, as if his head had been in the driver's lap. It happened to be a gay couple, and one of them was flaming, but they were okay, and they shared their pot with me. Shortly after this I go back to Florida and back to work with my best friend at the department store. The next year or so is spent working and partying as we went through a lot of Crown Royal while riding around snorting cocaine.

One night while out, we decided to stop at Denny's for breakfast. A friend who used to work with us at the department store was now a dishwasher at Denny's came out to socialize with us. Our waitress was an older lady who was in a foul mood and not very friendly, so after eating I unscrewed the cap to the saltshaker and turned the saltshaker upside down on the table with the cap on the top of the bottom and pushed it near the edge of the table.

We paid our bill quickly and got in the car and we were at the traffic light in front of the restaurant when we could see the waitress pick up the saltshaker and we could see her facial expression as she put her hands on her hips turned and yelled to the back for our buddy the dishwasher to come see what we had done, and we could see him just burst out laughing. How often do you get to see the results? Another night I was out with friends when they ran into a couple of girls they knew, and I ran into a guy I knew, he was the cousin of a friend. He told me he had just bought a Cadillac from his boss, so we took a ride in his new car and went to another bar where we picked up a couple of girls.

I was riding with one of the girls in her car as we followed my friend and the other girl in his Cadillac to her apartment when a police car pulled in the parking lot behind the Cadillac. As the police officer questioned my buddy, I could hear him ask for the registration, and when he could not produce the registration, I knew it was a stolen car. When the officer went to his car to call it in my friend took off running behind the apartment complex, and the officer called on the radio that the perpetrator had fled on foot.

When another cop showed up, we pointed to the back of the apartments and as the officer was running, he was pulling his gun out of his holster, and as he got to the corner of the building he took aim and shot my buddy in the shoulder. It turns out that my friend had waited behind the apartments to jump the officer and was trying to get the gun away from him when he was shot. The girls and I spent the night in the police station giving our statements. I would run into my friend a few years later at a party on the beach after he got out of jail, and he was still just as crazy as ever. On the way to The Who concert I was in the back seat of the car with my best friend and his girlfriend between us.

A good friend was driving, and his girlfriend was in the front seat with him, my best friend's girlfriend was cutting up some cocaine on a mirror in her lap when the driver accidentally hit his power window button. The driver's window went down a crack and the wind swirled the cocaine around and she bent over to cover it and yelled the driver's name so he would put his window up, when he did put his window up, she got up and the cocaine had been blown all over her lap. She was wearing very short shorts and the cocaine had gotten blown between her thighs and her shorts, my best friend and I took turns sticking the straw up her shorts to snort the coke out of her shorts. That was the best smelling cocaine of all time, talk about pink cocaine!

That was one of the best concerts of all time, because we were also tripping on acid. I think that was my last concert before I got married, and it was close to the time that I would meet my wife. I was out one night at a popular hot spot called the Brown Derby when I saw a woman with the most magnificent ass I had ever seen. I followed her out and saw her get in her car, so I got in my car and followed her. I got up beside her and was racing her until we got to the bridge where I got behind her and followed her home and asked her to go out with me, with a little badgering she said yes.

My relationship with her parents got off to a rocky start, it wasn't all my fault, but I still apologized and did my best to patch things up, but her parents still didn't come to our wedding even though we lived together for a year before we got married. One day we were at a party on the beach when one of my friends asked my best friend if he'd seen my wife's ass. She really did have the finest ass I ever had the pleasure to kiss, and she really loved sex in the beginning. We would never know when we'd be in the mood, hell we were always in the mood.

When we were first married, we lived in an apartment above a garage it had dark red and black curtains, carpet, sofa and bedspread. It was a very dark apartment, and we rescued a black cat that was part Manx, and I named him Spade. Between the dark apartment and my loud music Spade never had a chance, he was definitely a schizophrenic cat, one time he jumped on my bare back while I was doing dishes for no reason. It was around this time that my 13-year-old cousin was visiting, and she went to the beach on Sanibel Island with my wife and me.

While lying on the beach my wife and cousin go for a walk to go shelling on the beach, when they come running back saying they found something on the beach. When I go back with them it was what they said, a bale of marijuana had floated up on the beach and I wrapped it with a towel and put it behind a bush. Then I went to the car to get a blanket to wrap the bale with to make it easier to carry, but there were some police officers in the parking lot, and somebody had given them my description and I ended up getting arrested for constructive possession.

I paid a $500 fine and spent five years on probation. For finding something, not buying it. My wife told the police I had dollar signs in my eyes when she told me she found the bale. In the 60s and 70s this area was the largest import for marijuana in the country, shrimp boats would bring it in until they started using infrared detectors in airplanes and satellites that could detect an organic compound on a ship that was supposed to just have iced down shrimp.

When the Coast Guard would go out after the shrimp boats the shrimpers would throw the bales of weed overboard and the Coast Guard wouldn't get all of them. So sometimes after a storm a bale of weed would float up on the beach and someone would find it, dry it out, sell it and call it seaweed. There were T shirts with pictures of a bale marijuana with a fish head, fins, and tail that read "save the square grouper."

This is not the only time that I will be arrested while married. During the first few years of our marriage my wife will have to get me out of jail in every city we live in. It was because my license had been suspended for six years and I kept getting caught driving on a suspended license. Even though I had a North Carolina license I was not allowed to drive in Florida. I was still working for the department store at this point and for Christmas one year my wife and I both decided to get part time jobs with a catalog showroom.

The store manager for the catalog showroom lived in our apartment complex, and he talked me into applying for the assistant warehouse manager position, and I got the job. A department manager or assistant manager were working positions, but it was a job I was good at. I'd been unloading and loading trucks at the department store for a couple of years, so this was the same type of work I just had more responsibility than before, which included scheduling, doing employee evaluations and disciplinary actions. One day this cute 19-year-old female employee came into the warehouse office, her younger brother worked for me in the warehouse and had been put on probation for missing work without calling.

The female employee asked me if her brother was going to be fired, and I told her that was up to my manager, she then got very close to me and said, that if I would put in a good word for her brother, she'd be very grateful, as she put her hands on my hips and started to kiss me. I pushed her away saying I was married, and I said that wasn't necessary and I would talk to my manager on behalf of her brother. The warehouse manager did not fire her brother, and I had nothing to do with it. But this was just one example of opportunity presenting itself, this was the 80s and it was still dripping with sex.

The executive secretary of that store was one of the sexiest women I've ever known, short dark hair, with a beautiful, freckled face and a J-Lo ass. We flirted big time with each other, it never went anywhere though because we were friends. It wasn't too long before I was transferred to a store in the Tampa area, it was one of the stores that the catalog showroom had bought. The warehouses of these stores were total messes and took a lot of work.

While I was in Tampa, I was chosen to help open a new store's warehouse In Orlando, and I drove there and back daily for a week or two. One afternoon, or early evening I was driving home to Tampa when all these cars were pulled off on the side of the highway with the drivers standing outside their cars and looking to the east, and I could not understand what they were looking at. I then looked in my rearview mirror and saw this big orange ball of fire when I realized that it was the space shuttle being launched. I pulled over and got out of my car and watched, it was awesome.

It was probably 100 miles away but looked like it was just right there. It's an image that I will never forget, too bad it was before smartphones. There were a couple of girls in Tampa that I flirted with, one of them started kissing me on the loading dock when I licked my lips as I walked past her, one of my employees liked her, and was upset when he saw her kiss me. The other girl gave me a ride home one day when my car wouldn't start, it had just started to get dark on the way home when she pulled her car into the parking lot of a baseball park and turned off her car. She then told me that she had turned 18 two days earlier and was legal now as she grabbed my crotch, and I pushed her away telling her I was married.

She said she wouldn't take me home unless I let her suck me off, so I opened the door and started to get out she said, OK I'll take you home. She made me promise not to say anything to anybody about what happened and hoped that she hadn't jeopardized her job. Her job was safe, and I never said a word. My store manager in Tampa took me to a topless restaurant and made me swear not to tell anybody that we went. It wasn't too long after that I was promoted to warehouse manager and transferred to the store on North Miami beach. I showed up at my new store the night before I was scheduled to be there, and when I walked into the warehouse the employees were riding bicycles around shooting BB guns at each other.

There was merchandise laying all over the place, even underneath the big hydraulic receiving platforms. This was a small store in a mall with a small warehouse, but they wanted to stock everything that a regular warehouse would carry, including big items such as patio furniture, propane grills and lawn mowers. I worked my ass off for about a couple of months in that store, and the only adult employee I had was my receiver, but he only worked the mornings. My only other employees were part time high school students who could only work late afternoons and evenings, and my store manager would not let me fire or hire anybody.

I did catch one of my employees stealing, and that led to him, and two other employees being fired and arrested because they had thousands of dollars' worth of merchandise in their apartment. The assistant store manager was a creepy little guy, and one day he let me borrow his car. When I got into his car the seat and the floorboards were covered with McDonald's wrappers, when I pushed the wrappers off the front seat there were hundreds of roaches running around so I quickly got out of the car and took the keys back to the assistant manager and told him what I saw, and he just laughed about the roaches.

It wasn't long after this that my store manager gave me a list of merchandise to be shipped out by UPS that day. When I started pulling the merchandise, I noticed some of the stereo equipment was in boxes too big to ship by UPS. I called my store manager and told him the boxes were too big to go UPS and they'd have to go by common carrier, he told me to pull the mother fucking merchandise right god damn now and send it UPS. This store manager had a terrible temper and talked like this to his department managers all the time.

The assistant store manager called me a short time later to inform me that they were getting a common carrier to take the merchandise. It was after this I would quit the catalog showroom and go to work for an advertising company where I would work until my son was born. The advertising company did promotional work and had the Newport cigarette van that would drive around South Florida to give out sample packs of Newport cigarettes. I went with the Newport van when we took it to Key West for Fantasy Fest, which is like a mini-Mardi Gras. I was standing by the van giving out sample packs when this good-looking woman walked up, and she said she wanted my Newport T shirt that I was wearing.

I told her that I had other shirts in the van, but she said she wanted my shirt, when I asked her what I would wear if I gave her my shirt, she took off her shirt and gave it to me and was standing there braless with her beautiful petite tits staring me in the eyes. The following morning in Key West we were sitting on our motel balcony smoking cigarettes when a guy in jean shorts walked up to the pool shower, takes off his shorts and showers right next to a table where some old people are sitting having some coffee. Shortly after this we would leave Miami and go back to the West Coast of Florida. We got back when my son was about two weeks old, and after working a couple of odd jobs for about a year I applied for and got the job of receiving/ processing manager at a local discount store in town.

I had to go to Tampa for training, and in my hotel one night in Tampa my wife called to inform me that our cat Spade had died. He had been ill for a while with a urinary tract blockage and would just lay around on the bathroom floor urinating on himself until he died on the bathroom floor. My wife called the vet and he told her to put him in a plastic bag and bring him into the office the next morning, but before she put him in the plastic bag, she gave him a bath and blew him dry with a blow dryer to let him die with some dignity.

After training is over, I'm back unloading and loading trucks again. The last receiving manager this store had was not a very good manager and the department was a huge mess that I had to clean up. There was a 45-foot trailer full of clothing that had never been processed, and these stores were supposed to have 24-hour processing of their soft lines, and it took us about two weeks to get the truck full processed.

My department also had to put together the clothing fixtures and put them out on the floor for the soft line employees to fill. Shortly after this our store became number one in the region for soft lines, and even though it was my department that did most of the work the soft lines manager received all the credit. There were a couple of women I flirted with while I worked there, and one of them trapped me in the bedding stockroom until I forced her to let me out. She was so scared that I was going to turn her in, but I didn't.

I worked for this company for about a year and a half, and the operations manager was always on my ass. Whenever the trash compactor would need to be emptied, we would have to call the main office of Waste Management in Louisville Ky. Because Waste Management was having problems with their drivers, we could not get our compactor emptied and the operations manager fired me because of the buildup of trash in the compactor room. The store manager agreed to give me my vacation pay, and a two-week severance package and I went to work for my buddy who had his own fire sprinkler contractor service.

That was pretty hard work but good pay, but it didn't last very long. I would end up working a couple more jobs before we would leave Florida. One of the jobs was the delivery of and assembling waterbeds. The guy who worked with me was big and lazy. He was slow and very weak for his size.

He got fired when he lied to the boss about me not being able to handle the job. The spring before we left Florida my son who was a little over two years of age and I went to Plant City Florida for a Cincinnati Reds spring training game. My son who would watch baseball on TV with me would stand in the stadium aisle crouched over with his hands on his knees saying hey batter batter, and the fans around us got a kick out of him.

Even at the young age of 2 to 2 1/2 He could swing the wiffle ball bat and knock the hell out of a wiffle ball. It was around this time one day my son and I were getting ready to leave the house and we were on the back patio. My son was dressed in his Hawaiian shirt with his spiked hair and his sunglasses on when he decided to sit on the edge of the plastic wading pool. As he flipped over backwards into two feet of water, I got up quickly thinking that he would get up crying when he burst up out of the water laughing his little ass off.

That summer we would leave Florida with the intentions of moving to the northeast where my wife's mother lived. I worked for her stepfather for about a week, but we decided the area was too expensive, so we went and stayed with my mother in Louisville Ky. Before we left Florida, I had asked the authorities to let me off probation from when I found the bale of marijuana on the beach. They refused to let me off probation, but I left anyways.

Now in Louisville I was working nights doing the floors at Walmart when I got a speeding ticket. On a Saturday morning before I had a chance to pay the speeding ticket the police showed up at my mother's door with a warrant for my arrest because I had skipped probation. I was in jail for about a week until I was let out because Florida was not going to extradite me for what little time I had left on probation.

It was after this when I got a job at a gas station that was walking distance from my mother's place. With both of us working we put my son in a daycare, and the women that worked at the daycare had deep southern accents. Within two weeks my son sounded like a little southerner. While I worked at the station, I bought a 12-speed racing bike that I would ride with our neighbor who was a bodybuilder and a cop. As good of shape as he was in and being cocky as he was, he could not keep up with me on a bike.

While I was on my third or fourth job already in Louisville my wife got a job through an employment agency that she ended up working for 9 or 10 years. While working at the gas station I ended up meeting the owner and the general manager of a local roofing company, they hired me to do estimates and post job inspections. The general manager trained me in how to measure a roof and do post job inspections. During the slow winter months, I would work with the roofing crews to learn how the roofing work was done. One winter we decided to go to Florida for Christmas vacation and to a friend's house for a New Year's Eve party, where an old friend from school happened to be, the same guy that asked my best friend if he had seen my wife's ass at the party on the beach.

He asked me if I remembered when my Toyota Celica had been vandalized at a gas station years ago, and that I never found out who did it. He then admitted that it was him who had vandalized my car, and he said he did it because his girlfriend at the time told him that she had been fucking me. He said he was scared of me in school, but he wasn't scared of me anymore and if I wanted to fight, he would fight me. I laughed and said that was 15 or 20 years ago I'm not going to fight you over it. Soon after this the general manager of the roofing company would quit to go back to work for Owens Corning.

Shortly after that there was a huge hailstorm that covered all of metro Louisville and the surrounding areas. We were getting hundreds of calls a day for hail damage inspection and roofing estimates. We filed the estimates by zip codes so that I could grab areas that were close together and map out a route to start my day. This was before GPS when we had to use map books to find our way around.

I would go into the office at around 5:00 A.M., grab a bunch of estimates and map out a route to start my day. I would get a cup of coffee and be in front of my first house when it would get light enough to get on the roof. I would quietly stick one of my business cards in their door and put my ladder up to get on the house and measure up the roof. I got to where I could measure up 35 roofs by 12:00 to 1:00 P.M., then I'd go back to the office to do my math and write up the contracts for the secretary to type them up the next morning and mail them out. Our secretary who was married to one of our foremen and lived across the street from the office had a hot young daughter who would come over in skimpy clothing and flirt with me when I would be there in the evening by myself.

The secretary would send her son to bring her daughter home

because she knew I'd been drinking bourbon, and she knew how bad her 15-year-old daughter could be. I was relieved when the brother would show up to take her home because she was extremely hot! Before I came to work for this company the largest year in sales, they had was about 250,000, and in the first year after this hailstorm we did over 4,000,000 in sales two years in a row and three million a year for the next few years before we were averaging 1 to 2 million a year.

We had four crews paid by the hour when the hailstorm first hit, and we were getting hundreds of calls a day for estimates. Most of our roofers quit to go out on their own, and we had just enough roofers left to keep just one crew going. We tried hiring more roofers by running an ad in the paper offering the best wages in town, not one person showed up to put in an application. We then tried hiring local subcontractors who only wanted to work three or four guys on a crew, couldn't get a job completed in a timely manner, wouldn't show up on a Monday, but were there Friday for pay.

We then decided to hire crews from Texas which were Mexicans. The foremen of these crews from Texas had their papers and were legal, so we would pay the foreman for the job, and he would pay his workers. The guys from Texas would use as many guys as it would take to do a job in one day, or at least in a timely manner. When the storm first hit, and we were getting hundreds of calls a day we had a four-month backlog even though we eventually had 14 crews working for us.

We would have customers who signed a contract call us to tell us they didn't want any Mexicans on their roof, but that same customer would see one of our Mexican crews do a roof nearby and would say he wants that crew because they did an excellent job of clean up. As we caught up with the business from the hailstorm, most of the crews went back to Texas with the best crews staying on to do our regular work until another hailstorm bombarded Bowling Green Ky which is about 120 miles from Louisville. Because we opened an office there, the drive from Louisville to Bowling Green made for a stressful baseball season as I was driving back and forth for games and practices being that I was head coach. Between roofing and the roads, I saw more asphalt that spring than any I could remember.

We did a lot of business in a short amount of time in Bowling

Green and my boss gave me a nice bonus for it, my boss never really approved of me taking off work early for games or practices, but he was a family man and understood that my son came first. My son had started playing baseball around the time that I started for the roofing company, he didn't want to play t-ball, so he went right into the YMCA coach pitch league. the YMCA called me to be a head coach, so I did. The next year he played machine pitch, and the commissioner of the Babe Ruth league he played in called to ask me to be a head coach again. I told her that I didn't have much coaching experience and she said that that was OK, so I became a head coach again.

One little kid on my team who had a real strong arm was our best player, and he usually played third base. One day his father showed up for a game without him, and he explained to me that his son had to sign THE list at school that day, which is something bad they do at a Catholic school, and he had told his son that if he ever had to sign the list, he would not be able to play a game or practice that day. I then told the father that I understood his priorities, I then told him that I told my son that if he missed any grounders in the game he would have to stay home from school to practice.

We had a good laugh over that. Every year before tryouts the coaches would get together to grade each other's son, I would try to get my son graded as a third-round pick so I could get two picks before him. My son was a good ballplayer, just not one of the very best players in the league. After coaching for a couple of years I realized after the first few rounds of the draft to look for the kids with a "GLM," or "Good Looking Mom that is why it was a standing rule within the coaches that the mothers should be the ones to bring their sons to try out. Later in my son's baseball career when we were in kid pitch the head coach of the other team was having his son who was pitching quick pitch my batters.

Quick pitching is when you throw a pitch before the batter is ready, and in Babe Ruth baseball there is a rule against it and the umpire is supposed to control it. Well, the umpire was not controlling it, so I said something to the opposing coach about having his kid quick pitch my batters, and he said, "well Bub the kids got to learn to do it sometime My son would go on to play on a couple All Star teams one of which would go undefeated until the regionals which were held in Marinette Wisconsin, and even though my wife and I had separated a couple years earlier we rented a car and went to Wisconsin together.

The coach of this All-Star team that went to Wisconsin was one of the coaches I drank a lot of beer with after games at a local sports bar, or the occasional fish fry because a lot of the people in the league belong to the same parish, and I became an honorary Catholic. My son would go on to play a few more years of Babe Ruth baseball before I would put a little traveling team together that we had for a couple years. The scheduling of games, practices and getting uniforms was a lot of work but was also a lot of fun. It was a way to get the kids more competitive competition to get them prepared for high school ball.

I did not recruit kids other than ones that had played for me earlier, and I only scheduled the best competition. We would play around 40 games in just over two months; we would go to tournaments where we could play six to seven games in a weekend depending on how well we did. One tournament we went to in Cincinnati played games at a ball field where the concession stand sold beer. At this point I've been coaching for seven or eight years, and I'd never seen a Little League ballpark that sells beer.

The other team's parents had a few and were getting rowdy and rude. I had had a drunk father confront me after a game a few years earlier, but he had brought his own alcohol to the ballpark, and his breath smelled like bourbon. After a couple of years with the traveling team my son starts his high school career on the 9th grade team. The high school baseball program had a booster club that would use a bingo hall in town a couple of nights a week to raise money for the team, all the players and their parents would work bingo a couple nights a month, wearing aprons and selling scratch off tickets.

One night while working bingo with one of the "GLM" moms who I used to flirt with was flirting with me this night when I told her I was lucky to be wearing that apron. She had been the best looking "GLM" in that league, the problem was her husband was the best-looking guy in the league. The mother of one of my players worked for the Cincinnati Reds organization and I told her a story of when I was at Crosley Field for batting practice before a Reds game when Johnny

Bench was warming up about 15 feet away.

Me and about 10 other kids were yelling, "Mr. Bench come give me your autograph," repeatedly when Bench turned around and shouted, "why don't you fucking kids shut up and leave me alone She then told me that Bench is the ass of the organization, and nobody likes him. She then added, "but he was a great catcher My son's high school career only lasted into his freshman year as he quit the team and got a job because he wanted to buy a car and hang out with his friends. His mother and I had always told him that if he kept a "C" average in school, kept playing baseball, and held down a job we would buy him a car.

He quit baseball, was getting poor grades, but his mother bought him a car anyways because she didn't want to be his chauffeur. His mother did not see the importance of him continuing baseball. As I had said, his mother and I had separated a few years earlier with her telling me that she wanted a divorce. When she failed to file for the divorce, I told her I was going to file for custody. This prompted her to file, and we went to the courthouse to sign the papers together.

We did not own any property, so we wrote our own terms. In Kentucky when a divorce involves children, the parents and the children are supposed to attend a two-day class called "Families in Transition," the attorney that met us at the courthouse told us that because we had been separated for two to three years already that we probably wouldn't have to do "Families in Transition." After waiting for two or three months I called my wife to ask her what was taking so long. She then called me back to tell me she had talked to the attorney, and he told her that the judge would not sign off on the divorce until we did "Families in Transition. It took a couple of months for my wife my child and myself to complete the classes.

After waiting for what seemed like months and months, I called my wife to see what was taking so long. When she called me back, she said she found out why it was taking so long, she said that her attorney had diabetes, and had to have both of his legs amputated. I then said to her, "So he couldn't do the legwork," that's bad she said before laughing quietly. It was shortly after this that I received my divorce decree in the mail on Valentine's Day, so I called my wife to wish her a happy Valentine Day and told her the divorce decree was in the mail.

Several years earlier when we had first separated, I moved into an apartment on the third floor of an old house. It was in the older end of town, so the rent was cheap and there were three or four strip joints nearby. One of the strip joints became a regular hangout for me and I got to know a couple of the strippers. One of the strippers introduced me to threesomes and group sex. She liked to wear a strap on and introduced me to alternative styles of sex.

For the first few years after being separated my life was consumed with work, or my son. If it wasn't baseball or basketball season, we'd be at baseball mania training in the batting cages or with the pitching coaches. One winter he was in a hitting league where they would grade him on the quality of his hits. When the league was almost over, I made a bet with my son that he could not get a certain number of points, and that if he did get those points, I would have my hair bleached blonde.

On the very last day of the league, he got the points, and I had my aunt bleach my hair. My hair was fairly long and wavy so I should have had my aunt cut it before bleaching it, so now I have this long curly bleached blonde hair that my boss really hated, but my players and their parents loved the fact that I paid my bet. Bowling Green was a small town, so the hail damage business didn't last too long there, and my boss was unreasonable with his expectations. He could not understand why I could not do 30 to 35 estimates a day like I did after a hailstorm. It wasn't too long after this that I quit the roofing company and started a company of my own, in Kentucky and Indiana you don't need a license for roofing.

Every time the General Electric plant in Louisville would have a layoff there would be more roofers in Louisville. My company was going to be a general services company that included roofing, and did well for a couple years, but I was not good with the paperwork or the legal work, so I shut down the business and went back to work for the roofing company which didn't last very long so I sold cars for about six months before I went to work for Home Depot.

After working for the Home Depot for six months I decided to transfer to Fort Myers FL with the company.

I really thought that my son would end up following me back

to Florida, but he would meet a girl that would eventually become his wife and they would make their life in Louisville. I had already moved my mother back to Fort Myers a few years earlier, so my plan was to stay with her until I can get my own place. The Home Depot I went to work for was larger than the one in Louisville and was filthy in comparison. I worked in lumber and building materials and at night when cleaning up we would have to dust mop the floors.

I would take sawdust from the saws and spread some on the floor in front of the dust mop then spray the sawdust with water and push it around the floor to pick up the dust. When walking from the other end of the store it would look like lumber and building material floors were waxed. The store in Louisville had a higher standard when it came to cleaning so some of the employees of the store in Fort Myers were offended by my work ethic. Shortly before I left Kentucky, I had started having problems with my right arm and hand having numbness and pain.

When I went to the doctor in Fort Myers and had An MRI completed, he sent me to a neurosurgeon who told me I had a tumor in my spinal cord that he could not contend with and sent me to a cancer research and neurosurgery hospital in Tampa. The surgeon there found that the spinal cord was damaged but did not have a tumor. So, I ended up having surgery on my neck with eight or ten titanium pins and screws to re compress my spine. When the surgeon made the incision on the back of my neck, he cut the muscles that attach the shoulders causing me to have pain, weakness, and loss of motion in my arms and hands, I could barely even wipe my own ass.

After a couple of months of healing and physical therapy I went back to work at the Home Depot. Because of the weakness and range of motion loss the physical labor was a lot harder than previously, and I would spend more time driving a forklift. One day I was on a forklift loading a pallet of cement onto the back of a flatbed truck when I noticed the driver was wearing a Florida State Seminole hat. My being a Miami fan I asked him where on the bed he wanted it loaded, "wide left or wide right?" He did not like my comment at all. It takes a college football fan to understand the joke, Miami at one point beat Florida State in football five years in a row with a few of those games being lost with a last-minute field goal missing either wide left or wide right.

While working for the Home Depot I started a jet ski rental business and eventually quit the Home Depot. Jet skis at the beach at the time would cost $110 an hour to rent. So, I kept mine in a warehouse and would rent them out for a day or half day and meet the people at a boat ramp to launch and pick up. The business didn't last very long as the GWB economy nosedives, and the housing foreclosure crisis began. I ended up selling the jet skis and I got a job selling cars, then vacuum cleaners until I got a job driving an airport cab that ended up lasting 13 years. When I first got back to Florida, I fell back into my old lifestyle working and partying.

Even the surgery didn't slow me down, although it did take a couple months to heal up. It's easy to remember when I moved back down because it was Super Bowl Sunday 2004, so I was 45 and by the time I started driving the cab I was 47. After surgery I rescued a cat born to my best friend's cat which was an Apple Face Siamese, and the father was a big black and white tabby cat causing my cat to have a black mask with a white snout. My mother said one day while he was eating that he looked like a little raccoon, so I named him Rocky after The Beatles song "Rocky Raccoon."

After I am healed up from my surgery, and after my jet ski business failed, I was selling cars at a local dealership. While I'm selling cars my mother decided to move back to Louisville area and I must find another place to live. I got a room in Lehigh Acres for a couple months when my best friend asked me to move in with them in Cape Coral to help them out financially. I stayed with them for several months after starting with the cab company until another friend asks me to move into a house he owned, and his mother lived in. I lived there for about three years until his mother moved back to Indiana and the house would be in foreclosure. So Rocky and I move back across the river into Fort Myers where I found a nice one-bedroom apartment on the second floor right on the pool deck.

I was in that apartment for nine or ten years making it the longest place I have ever lived. When I moved in my rent was $600 a month which included water, and a washer and dryer. When I left my rent was $950 a month, and the airport cab business had been devastated by COVID. That is when I left Fort Myers and came back to Louisville to be near family. I have gotten a little ahead of myself, so let's go back a few years before I'll go back to Louisville.

I'll help move my mother from Bardstown Kentucky to Sun City center Florida. She was originally going to move back to Fort Myers until my brother hijacked her relocation because he was living near Tampa. When I first came back to Florida in 2004, I really thought it was right for me, and at first it was. Partying with my friends or just going to the beach and enjoying the sights.

Nighttime on the beach has always been one of my favorite places, especially if it is a dark beach with no dirty light. There are so many stars in the sky like being on a mountaintop at night. So many memories of making butt prints in the sand with girls from my younger years to a couple of women I would meet while vacationing on the beach with friends while I was living in Louisville. One of these women that I met on the beach was a friend of my best friend was 49 years old and recently divorced. The first night that we were together we went for a long walk on the beach until we were in a secluded spot.

When we finished making butt prints, she started crying and I was surprised to find out that I was just the second guy for her to ever be with. But I found that dating wasn't going to be easy having been stood up two or three times already since I was 40, so I would mostly just go out alone. Before I have surgery one night at a popular club on Fort Myers Beach there was this group of girls dancing and having a good time. The best looking of the bunch is a black girl who was 29 years old, but no one had asked her to dance.

So, I go over and ask her to dance, and when she gets up she is standing 6 feet 2 inches tall in her heels. I'm only 5 feet 4 Inches tall and as I'm looking up at her I am laughing to myself, she smiled and asked me if I still wanted to dance, while laughing I said, "yes, I'm glad it's not a slow dance." After a couple of dances, she invited me to join their group, and she told me that she was surprised that her height had not intimidated me, when I told her it was because I was only short in height. I ended up spending the night with her in her hotel room, and she was surprised that my penis was as big as it is, and circumcised.

She told me that I was the only white man she had ever been

with, and that she had only been with three other men who were 5'10" to 6'2" tall. I'm not huge but I am above average. On another night, this time after surgery I was at a gas station pumping gas around 1:00 o'clock in the morning when this woman walks up to me and says my name. She then says she was an ex-girlfriend of my high school best friend and tells me her name. When she told me her name I recognized her, but she looked like a crack whore, and she offered me some services if I would give her a ride.

I told her I would give her a ride, but I didn't need any services. One night after I had healed up from surgery I was at a nearby bar. I had struck up a conversation with a nice looking blonde and bought her some drinks when it was almost closing time she asked me for a ride home, in exchange for a blowjob. I agreed and we went out to get in my car.

On the way she said we couldn't go to her house because her boyfriend was home, so we went behind a shopping center to park when the police showed up and arrested us. They were originally going to charge her with prostitution, and they were going to charge me with solicitation, but ended up just being charged with loitering. I got out of jail the next morning and my best friend came and picked me up and took me to get my car out of impound.

Thankfully this is my last night ever spent in jail, and after the failure of my jet ski business within a few years of coming back to Florida I am driving the airport cab. Driving a cab was perfect for me because there was not a lot of physical labor to it, just lifting luggage in and out of the vehicle. I drove a 2007 Hyundai Santa Fe as a cab for seven years. When they took the Santa Fe out of service it had 440,000 miles on it, and it never had any motor or transmission work. My shift was 2 A.M. to 2:00 P.M .and I had Fridays and Saturdays off; those were my days off because I like college football.

Shortly after I moved back to Fort Myers into my one-bedroom apartment I was in the swimming pool after work one day. There was a woman present in a one-piece bathing suit with long blonde hair. She was a little on the heavy side, but with a nice figure and pretty face. We were in the deep end of the pool talking when she got close and put her knee in my crotch. We went up to my place where we each had a beer and made out for a little bit.

The next morning at work in my cab at 6:00 A.M. she called me asking me to come and fuck her right away. When I got to her apartment, she answered the door naked, now I don't want to sound shallow but that bathing suit she had been wearing held everything into place nicely. I couldn't get it up, you do have to be attracted to somebody to have sex don't you? I made up an excuse that it was me and not her then got out of there.

A couple of years later when I was in my early to mid-50s my boss hired a gorgeous 27-year-old woman to drive a cab. One morning in the cab lot at the airport she was crying in her cab. When I approached her to ask her if she was OK, she said that a customer had hit on her and that she was shaken up. I asked her if she needed a hug and gave her one and told her that is why you don't see many young, good looking female cab drivers.

I asked her if she'd like to go have lunch, but she said her boyfriend would not approve of her having lunch with some random hot dude. I told her I'm a 53-year-old guy, I'm not some hot dude. But I thanked her for the thought. We did end up dating for a couple of months when she broke up with her boyfriend, but they ended up getting back together. I loved driving a cab because, even though it was doing the same thing every day it was different people.

I would ask them if they saw any alligators while they were down, and most people would say they hadn't seen any. I would tell them that alligators are faster than a horse for about 40 yards, but if they ever got chased by an alligator, they didn't have to be faster than the alligator, they just had to be faster than whoever they were with. A few years before COVID hit an old girlfriend told me she was being evicted from her apartment so I told her she could come stay on my couch for a while and help me with my rent.

It was working out alright until she decided she wanted to bring her cat which did not please Rocky. Her cat was a long-haired orange tabby cat, and I don't think Rocky liked it because it reminded him of Donald Trump. Then she decided to bring her drug addled 29-year-old daughter to stay with us two different times. The second time she came to stay with us I was missing my deposit for work from the day before, it was only $48, and I would have given it to her if she had asked.

I told my friend that I wanted her daughter out by the time I got home from work and that I was going to renew my lease and I wanted her out by the end of the month also. Several years earlier when my first grandson is between one and two years of age I traveled to Kentucky and went to a Cincinnati Reds game on Father's Day with my father, my son, and my grandson making four generations together. That would also mark the 6th decade in which I've seen a game, regular season or spring training.

I've seen two World Series games, one in 1970 when the Reds lost to the Orioles. I also went to the first game of the 1990 World Series when they beat the Oakland Athletics in which I took my nephew who lived in Ohio but was an Oakland fan from the time that my brother and his family lived in San Francisco. It was the year after we had moved to Louisville and while I was working at the gas station. Cincinnati World Series tickets went on sale on a Saturday morning, and I kept hitting redial on the phone for 45 minutes before I had to go to work but never got through to buy tickets.

My wife kept hitting redial and got through and bought tickets by the time I got to work. You had to buy a ticket for each game that was in Cincinnati, so I bought two strips of 4 tickets, two seats for the four games in Cincinnati. The tickets cost $40 per seat, and I sold the two for the second game for $100 apiece. The Reds swept the series in Oakland, so I sent the four tickets for the last two games back and received a refund for those seats. I ended up making $40 and seeing the first game of the World Series.

Baseball is a common thread through my family, my father could have played pro baseball, but he wanted to be an Air Force pilot. A Brooklyn Dodger scout who watched my father play when he was in the Air Force gave my father 20 bucks, and his business card and told him to call when he got out of the Air Force. My father went on to have a 20-year Air Force career flying everything from B52s to an RF4 in Vietnam. My baseball career started when I can remember being on the field when my father coached my older brother's team until I was old enough to play on a team myself.

I played from the time I was six years old till I was 16, and I already told you about my son's career. Enough about baseball, so after my old girlfriend moved out It was just me and Rocky again. Still a year or two before COVID would hit and my boss at the cab company had bought some buses and had a couple of them cleaned up, serviced to use as shuttle buses between the local university and one of the malls, I agreed to drive one until he could find a regular driver. They were equipped with a handicap lift in the rear, and one evening I had just picked up some students in front of Target with one of them being in a wheelchair.

After riding up the lift with him instead of walking through the bus I decided to jump off the lift which was about four feet high. As soon as I jumped, I knew I had made a bad decision because as I landed my knees buckled as I fell forward and hit my head on one of the big red concrete balls in front of Target. It didn't knock me out, but it bloodied my forehead, and the store manager came out to check on me and brought me a wet rag. I went ahead and drove around the mall to drop students off and when I got back to target the store manager had called EMT and they checked me out for a concussion, but I was OK.

I went on to drive the bus for about a month until school was out. Once school was out, we would have a bit of a rush with families taking their summer vacations until August and September slow times would hit until the next tourist season would take off. But the next tourist season never took off because COVID killed it and I struggled until September of 2020 when I left Fort Myers and came back to Louisville to be with family.

Although my mother and my two brothers live in Florida my father, my son and his family, and my ex-wife who has helped me immensely since I came back all live in the Louisville area. Rocky stayed with my ex-wife because my dad did not want Rocky at his house. I stayed with my dad mostly and would stay with my ex-wife occasionally, until rocky and I got our own place. My aunt and uncle who were both in an assisted living home gave me her car because they weren't allowed to drive anymore. I had gotten a job at a department store in Louisville unloading trucks and stocking the sales floor with merchandise.

After driving a cab for 13 years the physical labor was a little overwhelming, and with the pain and numbness I had in my arms and hands since surgery in 2004 worsening I could not continue working. Luckily Kentucky is one state that opened their Medicaid program, so I was able to get medical coverage and went to the doctor. The doctor sent me to get an MRI done on my neck, and I ended up having surgery again.

After surgery I still have a lot of pain and numbness in my arms and hands and a lot of loss of motion. There's not as much pain but I can barely use my left hand and my right hand is not much better. So, I quit driving and sold my car, but not until after my grandsons' baseball seasons are over. Both of my grandfathers played baseball, so my grandsons are the 5th generation of my family to play baseball. I hope they both continue to play baseball, but with video games and other interests they may not.

It's 2022 now and Super Bowl 56 was a month or so ago, and the Rams won. I'm not a big NFL fan, I'm more of a college football fan but I like to follow my favorite college players that are in the NFL. My two favorite college teams are the University of Louisville, and the University of Miami Florida.

I'm not sure how to end this, So I'm going to use my last few lines to acknowledge my mother and father for never giving up on me. And for all the bridges I burned my family didn't let them burn down completely, for that I'm grateful. As for the friends and women that I used without realizing that is exactly what I was doing I am extremely sorry. My mother and father didn't raise me to be a misogynist, maybe it was society, or TV and the movies, but that is exactly what I was.

I still say things that are out of line, but now I will apologize for them. Even after realizing I needed to be a better person for my son, I never realized how offensive my behavior towards women was. I was never physically abusive to my ex-wife or other women, but I was mentally and emotionally abusive. Again, I apologize to my ex-wife and all the other women that I used. All I can do now is to be a better person than I was, and that shouldn't be too hard!

"About the Title"

This page is usually about the author, but you only must read the book to find out about me. The title of the book was going to be, "The Life and Times of a Modern-Day American Gypsy" Until my ex-wife said that the title should be, "You Know What You Ought to Do." She said this because that is a phrase that I use frequently when conversing with people followed by my opinion whether they had asked for it or not. As for why you should read this book, it is a compilation of bad decisions that take you on a trip into the fast-paced life of a military child, followed by a horrific car crash in high school, and being kidnapped in the Appalachian Mountains a few years later.

Then there is a year of college, a summer trip out west instead of going to summer school, and the ski trip to Europe by the time I'm 23. Married life came next, but it was fatherhood that eventually settled me down, although the bad decision making continued to make life harder than it needed to be. While the last 20 years of my life have been rather boring, I like to think that it is because the first forty plus years had more than a lifetime of memories already.

www.ingramcontent.com/pod-product-compliance
Lightning Source LLC
LaVergne TN
LVHW010508160826
845677LV00012B/2726

* 9 7 9 8 8 8 6 0 4 6 7 4 8 *